Quality Customer Service

How to Win with the Customer
Fourth Edition

William B. Martin, Ph.D.

A Fifty-Minute™ Series Book

Quality Customer Service

How to Win with the Customer

Fourth Edition

William B. Martin, Ph.D.

CREDITS:
Senior Editor: **Debbie Woodbury**
Copy Editor: **Charlotte Bosarge**
Production Manager: **Judy Petry**
Design: **Darin Stumme**
Production Artists: **Jake Yeagley, Darin Stumme**
Cartoonist: **Ralph Mapson**

© 1989, 1993, 2001 Crisp Publications, Inc.
Printed in the United States of America by Von Hoffmann Graphics, Inc.

CrispLearning.com

03 04   10 9 8 7 6 5

Library of Congress Catalog Card Number 00-108720
Martin, William B.
Quality Customer Service, Fourth Edition
How to Win with the Customer
ISBN 1-56052-599-1

This book is printed on recyclable paper with soy ink.

Learning Objectives For:

QUALITY CUSTOMER SERVICE

The objectives for *Quality Customer Service, Fourth Edition* are listed below. They have been developed to guide you, the reader, to the core issues covered in this book.

THE OBJECTIVES OF THIS BOOK ARE:

❑   1) To reveal the fundamentals of what it takes to win with the customer

❑   2) To describe what quality service is

❑   3) To identify service providers' winning customer service attitudes

❑   4) To explain how to identify customer needs

❑   5) To show how to provide for customer needs

❑   6) To explain how to ensure that customers return

ASSESSING YOUR PROGRESS

In addition to the learning objectives, Crisp Learning has developed an **assessment** that covers the fundamental information presented in this book. A 25-item, multiple-choice and true-false questionnaire allows the reader to evaluate his or her comprehension of the subject matter. To buy the assessment and answer key, go to www.crisplearning.com and search on the book title, or call 1-800-442-7477.

Assessments should not be used in any employee selection process.

About This Book

This book is for people who currently work, or plan to work, in a job that requires interaction with customers from outside of the organization as well as inside. It is addressed to front-line service providers who ultimately determine the quality level of customer service.

The premise of this book is twofold: 1) quality customer service is the key to success for any person with customer service responsibility, and 2) quality customer service is the foundation upon which an organization's success and profits are built.

Unfortunately, a majority of organizations today concentrate on the technical side of job performance and devote far too little time to the "people side" of business. Training is often catch-as-catch-can because of limited resources, busy schedules, and a lack of time. Also, many service supervisors are not experienced enough to properly train employees in effective customer relation skills. This program is useful for training new service providers as well as promoting the continued development of more experienced personnel. All that is required is an interested person, a pencil, and some time. *Quality Customer Service* and follow-up on the part of the manager or trainer will provide measurably improved customer service for any organization.

How to Use This Book

This *Fifty-Minute™ Series Book* is a unique, user-friendly product. As you read through the material, you will quickly experience the interactive nature of the book. There are numerous exercises, real world case studies, and examples that invite your opinion, as well as checklists, tips, and concise summaries that reinforce your understanding of the concepts presented.

A CrispLearning *Fifty-Minute™ Book* can be used in variety of ways. Individual self-study is one of the most common. However, many organizations use *Fifty-Minute* books for pre-study before a classroom training session. Other organizations use the books as a part of a system-wide learning program—supported by video and other media based on the content in the books. Still others work with CrispLearning to customize the material to meet their specific needs and reflect their culture. Regardless of how it is used, we hope you will join the more than 20 million satisfied learners worldwide who have completed a *Fifty-Minute Book*.

To The Reader

The person who gave you this book wants you to read it carefully, working all of the exercises and activities. If you have any problems as you proceed, ask your trainer/supervisor for assistance.

Once you have read the book and completed its exercises, you will be better prepared to practice the secrets of quality customer service. What you learn, and the subsequent changes this program brings, are far more important than the time it takes to finish. Read slowly and think about each point as it is introduced because it is there for you.

Interacting with customers should be fun and challenging. Ideally, you should enjoy interacting with the people with whom your job brings you in contact.

Dealing effectively with people requires many principles, methods, and skills which need to be recognized, learned, and practiced. Therefore, the way to make the most of your job is to enjoy it as fully as possible and learn all you can about the process. It is the combination of your attitude and your skills that will determine the kind of customer service you provide for your employer. *Quality Customer Service* can help make you a winner!

Good Luck!

William B. Martin

William B. Martin

P.S. It is a good idea to keep *Quality Customer Service* handy throughout your training as you may wish to refer to it for review.

Contents

Part 3: Notes and Comments

Is This Book for You?

To determine whether this book is for you, check (✔) "yes" or "no" for the following questions.

Does your job require you to interact with one or more of the following categories of people who depend on you for service?

Yes	No	
❏	❏	Clients
❏	❏	Customers
❏	❏	Constituents
❏	❏	Guests
❏	❏	Members
❏	❏	Passengers
❏	❏	Patients
❏	❏	Students
❏	❏	Other:_____

Does your job require you to interact with other people inside your organization who depend on you for service? These individuals may be called:

Yes	No	
❏	❏	Accounting
❏	❏	Boss
❏	❏	Co-workers
❏	❏	Engineering
❏	❏	Front-of-the-house
❏	❏	Marketing
❏	❏	Operations
❏	❏	Production
❏	❏	"The group down the hall"
❏	❏	"Those guys on the third floor"
❏	❏	Other:_____

If you checked "yes" for any of these questions, this book is for you.

PART 1

Winning with the Customer

2

Do You Have What It Takes to Win with the Customer?

The people in your organization think so, or they would not have hired you. Now is the time to prove them correct. Make your choice now!

Service Winners

➤ Those with a positive attitude and a cheerful outlook

➤ Those who genuinely enjoy working with and for other people

➤ Those with the ability to put the customer on "center stage" rather than themselves

➤ Those with a high energy level and who enjoy a fast pace

➤ Those who view their job primarily as a human relations profession

➤ Those who are flexible and enjoy new demands and experiences

➤ Those who can allow customers to be right (even on those occasions when they are not)

Add your own: _____

_____

_____

Service Failures

➤ Those who seem depressed or angry

➤ Those who would rather work alone or with "things"

➤ Those who need to be the center of attention

➤ Those who work at their own relaxed pace

➤ Those who consider technical aspects of the job more important than customer satisfaction

➤ Those who must have things happen in an orderly and predictable way

➤ Those who need others to know that they are right

Add your own: _____

_____

_____

The difference between winning and failing at customer service is a matter of sensitivity, sincerity, attitude and human relations skills—all of which can be learned.

It isn't enough to simply perform the duties of your job. You must also have the right approach.

➤ A patient in a doctor's office wants more than a treatment.

➤ Airline passengers want more than a safe flight.

➤ Clients in a transaction want more than a settlement.

➤ Customers in a restaurant want more than a meal.

➤ Guests in hotels want more than a room.

➤ Rental car customers want more than a car.

➤ Customers want more than just the product or service that is offered—they also want to be treated well!

Remember: Quality Customer Service winners are made, not born.

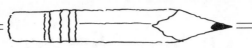

CUSTOMER SERVICE POTENTIAL SCALE

I control my moods most of the time.	10 9 8 7 6 5 4 3 2 1	I have limited control over my moods.
It is possible to be pleasant to people who are indifferent to me.	10 9 8 7 6 5 4 3 2 1	I simply can't be pleasant if people are not nice to me.
I like most people and enjoy meeting with others.	10 9 8 7 6 5 4 3 2 1	I have difficulties getting along with others.
I enjoy being of service to others.	10 9 8 7 6 5 4 3 2 1	People should help themselves.
I do not mind apologizing for mistakes even if I did not make them.	10 9 8 7 6 5 4 3 2 1	Apologizing for a mistake I didn't make is wrong.
I take pride in my ability to communicate verbally with others.	10 9 8 7 6 5 4 3 2 1	I would rather interact with others in writing.
I'm good at remembering names and faces, and make efforts to improve this skill when meeting others.	10 9 8 7 6 5 4 3 2 1	Why bother remembering a name or face if you will never see that person again?
Smiling comes naturally for me.	10 9 8 7 6 5 4 3 2 1	I am more serious by nature.
I like seeing others enjoy themselves.	10 9 8 7 6 5 4 3 2 1	I have no motives to please others, especially those I don't know.
I keep myself clean and well-groomed.	10 9 8 7 6 5 4 3 2 1	Being clean and well-groomed is not all that important.

Total score: _____

If you rated yourself 80 or above, you probably will be, or are, excellent with customers, clients, or guests. If you rated yourself between 50 and 80, you may need to learn better human relations skills before working with the public. If you scored under 50, working with customers is probably a poor career choice for you.

Comparing Customer Service to a Refrigerator

Customer service is *different from* a refrigerator because:

➤ You can't touch it.

➤ You can't open it up and look inside.

➤ It doesn't come in optional colors.

➤ You can't keep a supply in inventory.

➤ You can't even measure it precisely.

Most organizations deal in one way or another with tangible products or conditions. Like a refrigerator, these tangibles can be poked, prodded, weighed, or otherwise physically inspected. *Tangibles* often define the essence of what an organization is all about.

Some examples of organizational tangibles are:

Animals	Airplanes	Appliances
Automobiles	Buildings	Clothing
Computers	Contracts	Food
Germs	Guestrooms	Property
Minerals	Plants	Rockets

Practice

What are the tangibles that your organization deals with?

_____

_____

_____

Customer service is different—it is *intangible*.

Intangibles deal with the human side of an organization. They include human emotions, behaviors, understandings, feelings, and perceptions.

Intangibles are often elusive because you can't inspect, touch, or smell them to know whether they are "right" or "wrong." However, like a tangible product, intangible customer service is often the key to an organization's success.

Some examples of customer service intangibles are:

Accommodation	Attentiveness	Attitude
Anticipation	Flow	Guidance
Guarantee	Helpfulness	Knowledge
Satisfaction	Sensitivity	Tact
Timeliness	Tone	Understanding

Practice

What are some customer service intangibles that you have experienced?

_____

_____

_____

8

Customer service is also *like* a refrigerator because:

Producing a quality refrigerator requires:

- Care
- Communication
- Effort
- Feedback
- Knowledge
- Leadership
- Organization
- Planning
- Skill
- Systems
- And lots of practice

Producing quality customer service also requires:

- Care
- Communication
- Effort
- Feedback
- Knowledge
- Leadership
- Organization
- Planning
- Skill
- Systems
- And lots of practice

The same concerted effort that goes into creating a quality tangible product must be exerted toward customer service—if it is to achieve a designation of quality.

What Is Quality Customer Service?

Even though customer service is intangible and often elusive, it still can be seen, heard, and experienced. What counts is what customers see, hear, and experience.

Quality customer service can only be understood from a customer's perspective. We must define quality service through the eyes of your customers. Only when your customers perceive that you have delivered quality customer service have you done so.

Customers tend to rate the level of service that you provide from two dimensions:

> ➤ **The procedural dimension:** consists of the established systems and procedures to deliver products and/or service.

> ➤ **The personal dimension:** how service providers (using their attitudes, behaviors, and verbal skills) interact with customers.

From a customer's point of view, each dimension is critical to the delivery of quality service. The exercises and activities in this book reflect both dimensions of quality service.

QUALITY SERVICE EXERCISE

The diagrams below show the procedural and personal dimensions in graphic form. The vertical axis represents the degree of procedural service and the horizontal axis reflects a measure of personal service as seen by the customer. Study each diagram below. How would you describe the nature of the service reflected in each diagram? Indicate your responses in the spaces provided.

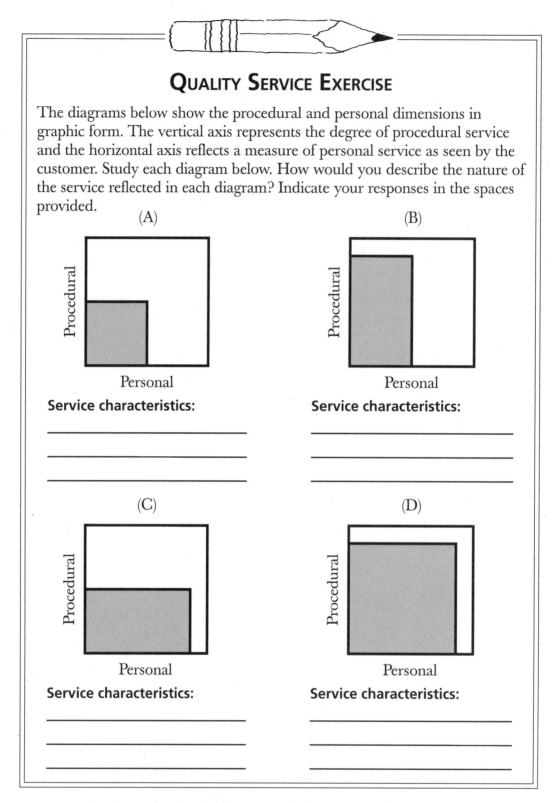

(A)

Procedural

Personal

Service characteristics:

_____

_____

_____

(B)

Procedural

Personal

Service characteristics:

_____

_____

_____

(C)

Procedural

Personal

Service characteristics:

_____

_____

_____

(D)

Procedural

Personal

Service characteristics:

_____

_____

_____

See the author's response to each diagram on the next page.

FOUR TYPES OF SERVICE

Diagram A:
The Freezer

This reflects an operation that is low in both personal and procedural service. This "freezer" approach to service communicates to customers, "We don't care."

Diagram B:
The Factory

This diagram represents proficient procedural service but a weakness in the personal dimension. This "factory" approach to service communicates to customers, "You are a number. We are here to process you."

Diagram C:
The Friendly Zoo

The "friendly zoo" approach to service is very personal but lacks procedural consistency. This type of service communicates to customers, "We are trying hard, but don't really know what we're doing."

Diagram D:
Quality Customer Service

This diagram represents quality customer service. It is strong in both the personal and procedural dimensions. It communicates to customers, "We care and we deliver."

(A)

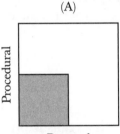

The "Freezer" service characteristics:

Procedural	**Personal**
slow	insensitive
inconsistent	cold or impersonal
disorganized	apathetic
chaotic	aloof
inconvenient	uninterested

Message to customers: **"We don't care."**

(B)

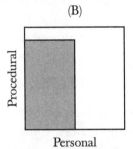

The "Factory" service characteristics:

Procedural	**Personal**
timely	insensitive
efficient	apathetic
uniform	aloof
	uninterested

Message to customers: **"You are a number. We are here to process you."**

(C)

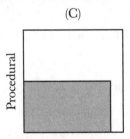

The "Friendly Zoo" service characteristics:

Procedural	**Personal**
slow	friendly
inconsistent	personable
disorganized	interested
chaotic	tactful

Message to customers: **"We are trying hard, but we don't really know what we're doing."**

(D)

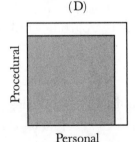

Quality Customer Service service characteristics:

Procedural	**Personal**
timely	friendly
efficient	personable
uniform	interested
	tactful

Message to customers: **"We care, and we deliver!"**

Four Reasons Why Quality Service Is Important

1 Service is where the money and jobs are.

There are more businesses providing services than ever before. The current top 10 largest growing jobs are all service-related. Moreover, the current top 10 industries with the fastest wage and salary employment growth are all service-related industries.

2 Increased competition.

Whether it's the corner gas station, Joe's Plumbing Service, a giant retail outlet, or an international bank, competition is keen. Business survival depends on obtaining the competitive edge. Quality customer service provides the competitive advantage for thousands of organizations.

3 Greater understanding of consumers.

We know more today than ever before about why customers patronize certain businesses and avoid others. Quality products, along with a realistic price, are a must—but that's not all. Customers also want to be treated well and will do repeat business with companies that emphasize service.

4 Quality customer service makes economic sense.

The lifeblood of any company is repeat business. Expanding the customer base is vital. This means companies not only have to attract new clients or customers, but also must keep existing ones. Quality customer service helps make this happen. Following is a partial list of organizations that benefit from "quality customer service."

Hotels	Banks	Restaurants/supermarkets
Insurance companies	Libraries	Construction/utility companies
Health facilities	Lawyers' offices	Doctor's offices/hospitals
Universities/clubs	Security services	Travel/tour-related businesses
Service/repair companies	Retail stores	Federal/state agencies

Is your type of organization represented above? Should it be?

Adopting a Customer Service Perspective

"The customer is king."

"The customer is the reason we exist."

"Without our customers we have nothing."

"Our customers define our business."

"If we don't understand our customers, we don't understand our business."

Each of these statements reflects a customer orientation—a view that the customer is paramount to the nature and success of one's organization—a view that turns the traditional view of organizations literally upside down. This view is the customer service perspective.

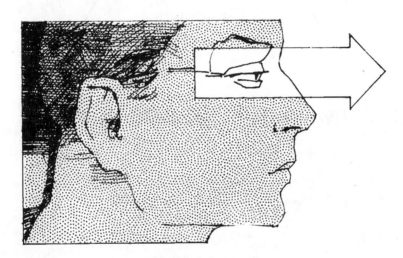

Adopting a customer service perspective requires us to look at organizations in a unique way. A view of customer service maintains that the most important activity in which the organization engages is the point in time when the organization's service provider interacts with the customer.

In short, this is customer service's defining moment:

➤ This is the essence, the heart and soul, of customer service.

➤ This is the point-of-service encounter.

➤ This is what Jan Carlzon of Scandinavian Airlines has succinctly labeled, "The Moment of Truth."

The Traditional Perspective

The Customer Service Perspective

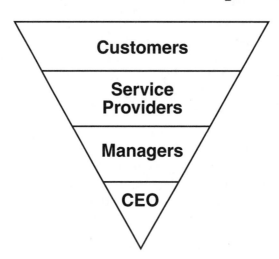

SERVICE ROLES EXERCISE

Here is an organizational diagram representing a customer service perspective:

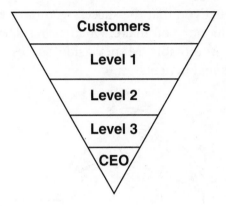

Answer the following questions as they pertain to your job.

1. In the organization where you work, who are the Level 1 people?

2. Who are the level 2 and 3 people?

3. Who is the CEO?

4. What is the role of the Level 1 service providers?

5. What is the role of the managers?

6. What is the role of the CEO?

Why Winning at Customer Service Is Important to You

Common sense should tell you that the success you have with customers will increase the amount of money you make, whether in salary increases or tips, as well as make you more promotable. Money aside, success in customer relations also provides many personal benefits.

MY CURRENT SITUATION

Read each statement below. Determine which are true and which are false about the benefits good customer relations skills can bring to you, then compare your answers with those of the author at the bottom of the page.

True or False?

❏ T   ❏ F   1. Working with customers is usually more enjoyable than working at a routine technical job.

❏ T   ❏ F   2. Improving interpersonal skills can help develop a personality.

❏ T   ❏ F   3. The ability to provide the best possible customer service is a continuous challenge that keeps a job interesting.

❏ T   ❏ F   4. Most top executives lack effective customer relations skills.

❏ T   ❏ F   5. Ongoing success with customers can lead to better job security and opportunity for promotion.

❏ T   ❏ F   6. Learning to treat customers as special people has a "carry-over" value to future jobs.

❏ T   ❏ F   7. What you learn about customer/client services in an entry level position is often more important than the money you make.

❏ T   ❏ F   8. Service jobs where you meet the public are easier than most technical jobs.

❏ T   ❏ F   9. Skill in performing the mechanics of your job is more important than your attitude about how you perform it.

❏ T   ❏ F   10. Smiles are contagious.

Answers: 1.T 2.T 3.T 4.F (Many top executives use effective guest relations skills to get them to the top.) 5.T 6.T 7.T 8.F (Guest relations jobs are more demanding because they require you to stay positive all the time.) 9. F (Your attitude is at least as important as your job skills.) 10.T

Four Steps to Quality Customer Service

Quality Customer Service

There are four steps in the process of winning with the customer.

STEP **1** Transmit a Positive Attitude

STEP **2** Identify Customer Needs

STEP **3** Provide for the Needs of Your Customers

STEP **4** Make Sure Your Customers Return

STEP 1 TRANSMIT A POSITIVE ATTITUDE

An attitude is a state of mind influenced by feelings, thought, and action tendencies. The attitude you send out is usually the attitude you get back.

Most customer service providers who fail do so because of attitude. If you don't make a good initial impression on customers, clients, or guests, the game is over before it begins. Sending a positive attitude to all with whom you come in contact is essential to quality customer service.

Alison was a disagreeable sort. Her fellow workers at the supermarket where she was a checker found her moody. Customers did not appreciate her sour disposition, and a few said so to the manager. When business took a temporary downswing, it came as no surprise when Alison was the first to be laid off.

HOW POSITIVE IS YOUR ATTITUDE?

The attitude you project to others depends primarily on the way you look at your job. To measure your attitude toward others, complete this exercise. Circle the extent you agree or disagree with each statement.

		Agree				Disagree
1.	There is nothing demeaning about assisting or serving others.	5	4	3	2	1
2.	I can be cheerful and positive to everyone regardless of age or appearance.	5	4	3	2	1
3.	On bad days when nothing goes right, I can still find ways to be positive.	5	4	3	2	1
4.	The higher the quality of service I provide during work, the better I feel.	5	4	3	2	1
5.	I am enthusiastic about my job.	5	4	3	2	1
6.	Encountering difficult "people situations" from time to time will not cause me to be negative.	5	4	3	2	1
7.	The idea of being a professional at customer contact is motivating.	5	4	3	2	1
8.	Performing a "people-oriented" job is both challenging and fun.	5	4	3	2	1
9.	It gives me great pleasure when others compliment me or my organization for superior service.	5	4	3	2	1
10.	Doing well in all aspects of my job is very important to me.	5	4	3	2	1

Total _____

If you scored above 40, you have an excellent attitude toward your job. If you scored between 25 and 40, you seem to have some reservations that should be examined before you make a career which involves customer contact. A rating below 25 indicates a non-customer relations job would probably be best for you.

TRANSMIT A POSITIVE ATTITUDE
Be Attentive to Your Appearance

You never get a second chance to create a positive first impression.

First impressions are critical because there may be no opportunity for a second impression!

Communicating Your Best Image

Like an actor or actress, interacting with others requires you to be on stage at all times. Creating a good first impression is essential. It is also important to understand that there is a direct connection between how you look to yourself and your attitude. The better your self-image when you encounter customers, clients, or guests, the more positive you will be.

ARE YOU COMMUNICATING YOUR BEST IMAGE?

Rate yourself on each grooming area presented below. If you circle a 5 you are saying that improvement is not required. If you circle a 1, you need considerable improvement. Be honest with yourself.

5 = Excellent 3 = Good 1 = Poor

Hairstyle, hair grooming (appropriate length & cleanliness)	5	4	3	2	1
Personal habits of cleanliness (body)	5	4	3	2	1
Personal habits of cleanliness (hands, fingernails and teeth)	5	4	3	2	1
Clothing and jewelry (appropriate to the situation)	5	4	3	2	1
Neatness (shoes shined, clothes clean, well pressed, etc.)	5	4	3	2	1
General grooming: Will your appearance reflect professionalism on the job?	5	4	3	2	1

When in comes to appearance on the job, I would rate myself:

❏ Excellent   ❏ Good   ❏ Need Improvement

The most successful people in customer contact jobs claim that to be sharp mentally means communicating a positive self-image.

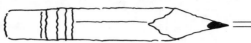

BODY LANGUAGE AND ATTITUDE

Did you know that body language can account for more than half of the message you communicate? Here is a body language checklist. Place a check (✔) in the square if you can answer "yes" to the question.

❑ Do you hold your head high and steady?

❑ Do your arms move in a natural, unaffected manner?

❑ Are your facial muscles relaxed and under control?

❑ Do you find it easy to maintain a natural smile?

❑ Is your body movement controlled, neither harried nor too casual?

❑ Do you find it easy to maintain eye contact with people you are talking to?

BODY LANGUAGE EXERCISE

Four sets of opposite nonverbal messages are presented below. Can you describe the possible messages these forms of body language send to guests?

Positive Messages	**Negative Messages**

Face is relaxed and under control.

This communicates: _____

_____

_____

Face is anxious and uptight.

This communicates: _____

_____

_____

Smile is natural and comfortable.

This communicates: _____

_____

_____

Smile is missing or forced.

This communicates: _____

_____

_____

Eye contact is maintained when talking and listening to others.

This communicates: _____

_____

_____

Eye contact is avoided when talking and listening.

This communicates: _____

_____

_____

Body movement is relaxed, yet deliberate and controlled.

This communicates: _____

_____

_____

Body movement is harried and rushed.

This communicates: _____

_____

_____

Compare your comments with those of the author on page 103.

TRANSMIT A POSITIVE ATTITUDE
Monitor the Sound of Your Voice

The tone of your voice, or how you say something, is often more important than the words you use.

Charley is a 10-year veteran on the local police force. As a patrolman in one of the toughest parts of town, he developed an authoritarian and intimidating tone to his voice. Now that Charley has been transferred to community affairs, he has had to learn to adjust his voice to project a more conciliatory and friendly image.

How Well Do You Use Your Voice?

The tone of voice you use with others may mean the difference between acceptable job success and great job success, between adequate customer service and quality customer service.

Below are different voice styles by which people communicate. Which seem to best describe yours? Check (✔) the one(s) with which you identify most.

- ❏ **My voice becomes agitated and/or loud when I am angry.**

- ❏ **I speak more quickly when nervous.**

- ❏ **My voice slows significantly and/or becomes quieter when I get tired.**

- ❏ **Others describe my tone of voice as "upbeat."**

- ❏ **Friends regard my tone of voice as warm and understanding when we are in a serious conversation.**

- ❏ **I can control my tone of voice in most situations.**

- ❏ **My voice can sound authoritarian and demanding when required.**

- ❏ **Others consider my voice meek.**

- ❏ **I'm lucky because my voice is clear, direct, and natural.**

- ❏ **My vocabulary and style of speaking tends to be serious and scholarly.**

- ❏ **Some of the above are better than others when interacting with customers.**

Please review the comments of the author on page 103.

Note: This may be a difficult exercise for those not accustomed to listening to themselves. Ask a friend to help you complete this exercise; it may provide some invaluable insights. Use of a tape recorder or telephone answering device can also be helpful.

TRANSMIT A POSITIVE ATTITUDE
Use the Telephone Effectively

Skill on the telephone is important because:

1. You have only your voice to rely on. Body language, written messages, and visual aids are unavailable.

2. When you are on the phone with a customer or client, you are the single representative of your company. In other words, you *are* your organization.

Question: True or False? When you answer the phone with a smile on your face, the tone of your voice will communicate a positive attitude to the person calling you.

True or False?

Answer: True

How Well Do You Use the Telephone?

Treating customers professionally means being as pleasant over the phone as you are in person. Take the telephone quiz below and see if you can score 100%.

True or False?

❏ T   ❏ F   1. It is okay to keep someone waiting on the phone while you attend to another equally important task.

❏ T   ❏ F   2. You should actually smile when you answer the telephone.

❏ T   ❏ F   3. If nobody is around to answer a ringing phone and it is not your assigned job, the best thing to do is to let it ring.

❏ T   ❏ F   4. It is acceptable to not return a call. If the call was important, the calling party will try again.

❏ T   ❏ F   5. If a customer is rude, it is your right to be equally snippy.

❏ T   ❏ F   6. You should identify yourself by name when answering a business related telephone call.

❏ T   ❏ F   7. If business is slow, it is perfectly acceptable to make personal calls to your friends.

❏ T   ❏ F   8. It is important to communicate a sincere interest in the caller and the information that is being requested or provided.

❏ T   ❏ F   9. The conversation should be ended in a upbeat manner, with a summary of any action to be taken.

❏ T   ❏ F   10. When you are upset, it is possible to communicate a negative attitude over the phone without realizing it.

Answers: 1. F 2. T 3. F 4. F 5. F 6. T 7. F 8. T 9. T 10. T

TRANSMIT A POSITIVE ATTITUDE
Stay Energized

Customer Service Myths

1. Customer service is less tiring than other jobs that require hard physical labor.

2. Providing quality customer service every day—all the time—is easy.

3. If you can be helpful and friendly to one customer, then you will find it just as easy to treat hundreds of customers the same way.

Customer Service Realities

1. Customer service requires the exertion of emotional labor. Emotional labor takes its toll on your energy level just like physical labor does; that is, it makes you tired.

2. The ideas and concepts presented in this book are simple to understand. But that does not mean that they are necessarily easy to accomplish every day all the time. Providing quality customer service on a regular basis can be very challenging.

3. Serving many customers over an extended period of time can be very tiring. When you have exhausted your reservoir of emotional energy, it is called *contact overload syndrome*.

How Well Do You Handle Contact Overload?

We all need our batteries charged from time to time! Your ability to re-energize yourself is important to maintaining a positive attitude toward your customers. Maintaining your positive attitude is your key to delivering quality customer service every minute on the job. Answer the following questions.

1. Is contact overload syndrome a potential problem for you?

❏ yes   ❏ no

If so, how? _____

_____

_____

_____

_____

_____

2. When you are emotionally tired, what can you do to re-energize yourself? _____

_____

_____

_____

_____

_____

Signs of Contact Overload

When you are suffering from contact overload you can become:

➤ tired

➤ listless

➤ dejected

➤ grouchy/impatient

➤ clumsy

Each one of these conditions reduces your ability to provide quality customer service.

Remember:

➤ Customer relations is an integral part of your job—not just an extension of it.

➤ Nothing is more important to your company than customers. Without them, your company could not exist.

➤ Satisfied customers are essential to the success of your organization.

➤ Business grows through satisfied customers. Satisfied customers not only come back, but they also bring their friends.

➤ Quality customer care is learned—not inherited.

➤ Like mastering any skill, being able to excel in customer care requires practice and experience. The more you put into it, the more you will receive from it.

> *In other companies where I have worked, the maintenance departments made me feel guilty about calling them for help. But here, the people in maintenance are a joy to work with. No matter what time of day or night, no matter what the problem is, they are always smiling and willing to help. That sure makes my job a lot easier."*

–Office Worker

CASE STUDY: THELMA'S PERFORMANCE APPRAISAL

Thelma works in a fast-food restaurant as a counter person. Here is what Thelma's manager had to say on her last performance appraisal:

"Thelma is extremely conscientious about getting her work done. She follows the outlined procedures exactly. She can be relied upon to get a job done quickly and efficiently. She often works overtime and does so without complaining. She is a hard worker who strives to do the technical part of her job right, and is highly productive.

However, when it comes to interacting with customers, Thelma needs considerable improvement. She often fails to see their point of view or consider their feelings. She sometimes acts like customers are an irritation interrupting her work. She is regarded by some as uncaring and tends to be inflexible when they request extra service.

If her performance continues, it will be necessary to reposition Thelma to the kitchen where customer contact is limited."

CASE STUDY QUESTIONS

1. Is Thelma a good employee? ❏ yes ❏ no
Explain: _____

_____

_____

2. Is the manager justified in his recommendations? ❏ yes ❏ no
Why or why not?_____

_____

_____

3. What suggestions would you make to Thelma?

_____

_____

_____

See the author's comments on page 103.

TRANSMIT A POSITIVE ATTITUDE
Summary and Follow-Up

Summary

Reflecting a positive attitude on your job is nothing more than really liking your job and allowing your actions and words to broadcast this enjoyment to your customers, supervisors, and fellow employees.

Positive attitudes are shown in:

➤ Your appearance

➤ Your body language

➤ The sound of your voice

➤ Your telephone skills

Make sure all of these reflect a positive attitude from you and check each one that still needs work on your part. Practice makes perfect.

38

Follow-Up

You have now completed Step 1 of this program. This is a good time to sit down with your manager and/or trainer and talk about what you have learned. This is also a good time to clarify any questions you may have about the job. Tell your manager you have completed this section and arrange a meeting. Use the space below to make notes about what you want to talk about and/or your questions.

THINGS TO DISCUSS:

1. Questions to my manager about our customers:

_____

_____

2. Questions to co-workers about procedures and routines:

_____

_____

3. Some of my ideas:

_____

_____

4. Follow-up based on discussion:

_____

_____

5. Other:

_____

_____

STEP 2 IDENTIFY CUSTOMER NEEDS

When serving customers, guests, or clients, it is important for you to know:

➤ Who your customers are

➤ What your customers want

➤ What your customers need

➤ What your customers think

➤ What your customers feel

➤ Whether your customers are satisfied

➤ Whether your customers will return

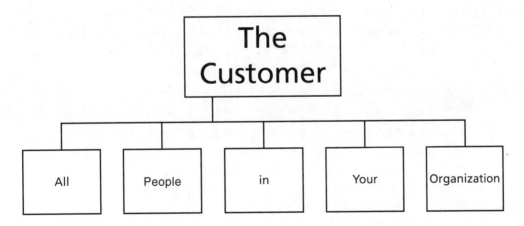

Chain of command: The customer is the boss.

Customers come in two varieties:

➤ External

➤ Internal

External customers are people outside of your organization who depend on you for service, and are doing business with you because they have chosen to.

A targeted group of customers is part of what is commonly referred to as an organization's market niche. This targeted group of customers has its own differing service needs, wants, and expectations. You cannot provide quality service without fully realizing what it is that your external customers need and want. If you don't, they will most likely choose to do business with someone else.

Internal customers are people inside of your organization who depend on you for service, and may have little or no choice when it comes to receiving service from you.

Internal customers may be co-workers, your boss, or people in another department within your organization. They also have differing service needs, wants, and expectations. You cannot provide quality service without fully realizing what it is that your internal customers need and want. If you don't, your degree of success in your organization will most likely be very limited.

> ❝ *Each of my major divisions is a service provider for the other divisions. For example, engineering must design parts that meet the needs of production. The production division must gear up to meet the orders from marketing. And the marketing division must keep engineering informed of changes in the marketplace. So you see, we all provide service to each other."*
>
> **—A Corporate CEO**

DEVELOPING A CUSTOMER PROFILE

This exercise will help you develop a profile of your customers, both internal and external.

Describe your customers (age, gender, other characteristics):

Internal: _____

External: _____

What is important to them?

Internal: _____

External: _____

What do they like?

Internal: _____

External: _____

What do they expect from you?

Internal: _____

External: _____

How do they view you?

Internal: _____

External: _____

Now that you have identified who your customers are and have developed a preliminary profile of what they like, what is important to them, and what they want from you, it is time to investigate what they may *need* from you.

HUMAN NEEDS

Customer needs are service imperatives. It is necessary to satisfy a service need before the service encounter can be considered successful or one of quality. Following is a list of common human needs. Check (✔) those that reflect the needs of your customers, guests, or clients.

- ❑ **The need to feel welcome.**
- ❑ **The need for timely service.**
- ❑ **The need to feel comfortable.**
- ❑ **The need for orderly service.**
- ❑ **The need to be understood.**
- ❑ **The need to receive help or assistance.**
- ❑ **The need to feel important.**
- ❑ **The need to be appreciated.**
- ❑ **The need to be recognized or remembered.**
- ❑ **The need for respect.**

Give yourself a perfect score if you checked all 10 items. All customers, regardless of your business or operation, have these basic human needs to some degree or another.

IDENTIFY CUSTOMER NEEDS
Understand Basic Needs

Just like you, customers, guests, and clients need:

➤ help

➤ respect

➤ comfort

➤ empathy

➤ satisfaction

➤ support

➤ a friendly face

Reading the Customer Requires Empathy

Empathy is what understanding is all about. This means putting yourself in the position of your customers. You must view the situation through "their eyes." You must ask, "If I were this person, what would I want?"

Practice

Do you have the ability to be empathetic to your customers, clients, or guests?

❏ yes   ❏ no

Why do you think so? _____

_____

Four Basic Needs

1. The Need to Be Understood

Those who select your service need to feel they are communicating effectively. This means the messages they send should be interpreted correctly. Emotions or language barriers can get in the way of proper understanding.

2. The Need to Feel Welcome

Anyone doing business with you who feels like an outsider will not return. People need to feel you are happy to see them and that their business is important to you.

3. The Need to Feel Important

Ego and self-esteem are powerful human needs. We all like to feel important. Anything you can do to make a customer feel special is a step in the right direction.

4. The Need for Comfort

Customers need physical comfort—a place to wait, rest, talk, or do business. They also need psychological comfort—the assurance they will be taken care of properly, and the confidence you will meet their needs.

IDENTIFY CUSTOMER NEEDS
Be Aware of Timing Requirements

Harry is a sales manager at a large auto dealership. Since the dealer makes money from the service department, Harry plays a crucial role in the overall success of the company. One thing that Harry has done to build new business and convert it to repeat business is develop a new system to expedite the taking of service orders first thing in the morning. Since most customers drop their car off on the way to work, getting customers processed as quickly as possible is important. Meeting his customers' timing needs is just one way Harry has built his service department into the busiest one in the area.

How Timely Should You Be?

Knowing the service time requirements for your operation is critical to performing quality service.

Five important personal contact points are listed below. There is also space for you or your manager/trainer to add additional items specific to your situation. Indicate what you think the response time should be for each item in the blank provided. Then, ask your supervisor or trainer to do the same. Once you have completed the exercise, try to arrange a meeting to discuss the timing needs of your job with your trainer or supervisor.

Personal Contact Point	Your Response	Supervisor's Response
1. A customer approaches the service area. The customer should be greeted, or have his/her presence acknowledged within _____ seconds.	_____	_____
2. Completing the initial paperwork or transaction should be completed within _____ minutes.	_____	_____
3. Any follow-up paperwork or transaction should be completed within _____minutes.	_____	_____
4. Special requests should be handled within_____ minutes or the guest, customer, or client should be notified of the reason for the delay.	_____	_____
5. Telephone calls should be answered within _____rings.		
6. Other; specify _____		
_____	_____	_____

See comments of author on page 104.

IDENTIFY CUSTOMER NEEDS

Stay One Step Ahead of Your Customers

> *Proper anticipation is the key to my day-to-day success.*
> *Without it, I'm out of business in no time."*
>
> **—A Restaurant Manager**

Anticipate the needs of your customers, clients, or guests. Ask yourself:

"Have I considered all of the customer's needs?"

"What will the guest need next?"

"How can I improve service now for my client?"

Then, offer or provide that service, without requiring a customer to ask for it!

Bob and Ruth are nurses. They work for a different doctor at the same medical clinic. Before each day begins, Ruth goes over the appointment list and makes sure potentially needed supplies, equipment, and medication are at her immediate disposal. Bob, on the other hand, attends to his patients' needs as they are treated. It is not surprising that Ruth finishes her patient load long before Bob.

How Well Do You Anticipate Customer Needs?

Five common service situations are listed below. After each, write in the space provided what you think is needed next.

After you complete the five specified situations, add some of your own, or ask your supervisor/trainer to add to the list.

Situation   **Anticipated Need**

1. A customer has waited longer than normal
   for service.   _____

                                                  _____

2. The client keeps glancing at his watch.   _____

                                                  _____

3. A woman guest with three small children
   approaches your service area.   _____

                                                  _____

4. Lines for your service form early in the day. _____

                                                  _____

5. There are well-defined busy periods in your
   workday.   _____

                                                  _____

Others needs specific to your situation:

_____   _____

_____   _____

_____   _____

_____   _____

See author's comments on page 104.

IDENTIFY CUSTOMER NEEDS
Remain Attentive

Attentiveness is the skill of understanding what your customers may need and want. This goes beyond timeliness and anticipation and requires you to tune in to the human needs of your customers.

How Well Do You Read Your Customers?

Reading the customer requires sensitivity. Reading the customer requires being sensitive to both nonverbal and verbal signals that customers send out (sometimes without being aware). Here are some common signals. Can you think of customer needs that the following signals might be communicating?

Signal		Possible Customer Need
Age of customer:	Young	_____
	Elderly	_____
Type of Clothing:	High fashion	_____
	Out-of-fashion	_____
	Worn out	_____
Verbal ability:	Extremely fluent	_____
	Barely fluent	_____
Attitude:	Positive	_____
	Negative	_____
Impatient:		_____
Demanding or angry:		_____

Compare your comments with those of the author on page 104.

HOW DO YOUR CUSTOMERS
SIGNAL THESE NEEDS TO YOU?

To help you identify when your customers have one or more of these basic needs, indicate below what customers do or say that serve as a signal that one or more "needs" requires your attention.

What your customers might do or say
to signal a basic need: **Message**

_____

_____ } → "I need to be understood."

_____

_____

_____ } → "I need to feel welcome!"

_____

_____

_____ } → "I need to feel important."

_____

_____

_____ } → "I need to feel comfortable."

_____

See the author's comments on what customers commonly do and say
to signal each of these basic needs on page 105.

IDENTIFY CUSTOMER NEEDS
Practice Skillful Listening

> **"** *The most important activity any company can do is listen to its customers. Listen hard and listen well—that is the secret to financial success."*

—**A Management Consultant**

Five ways to be a better listener:

1. Stop talking

2. Avoid distractions

3. Concentrate on what the other person is saying

4. Look for the "real" meaning

5. Provide feedback to the sender

Lisa works in the reservations office of a hotel. She arrives early each morning to take reservations over the telephone. Lisa always repeats the date of arrival and number of nights of the reservation back to the caller and waits for confirmation. Her listening skills help keep mistakes at a minimum and customers happy.

WHAT DO YOU KNOW ABOUT LISTENING SKILLS?

Ten faulty assumptions about listening are listed below. Read each carefully and check (✔) ones that you have previously held. Don't forget to read carefully the correct assumptions about listening.

Faulty Assumptions

❏ 1. We learn to listen automatically; training is unnecessary.

❏ 2. Listening ability depends on intelligence.

❏ 3. Listening ability is closely related to hearing acuity.

❏ 4. Generally, most of us can listen well and read something else at the same time.

❏ 5. We listen well most of the time.

❏ 6. What we hear is usually what was said.

❏ 7. Listening is a passive action.

❏ 8. Personality has little effect on listening ability.

❏ 9. Listening is done only through the ears.

❏ 10. Listening should be concerned with content first and feelings second.

CORRECT ASSUMPTIONS

1. Effective listening is a skill that is difficult for most of us. Practice and training can improve our ability to listen well.

2. There is no relationship between intelligence and listening skill.

3. Ability to hear is a physical phenomenon. It has little to do with our ability to listen. In fact, people with hearing loss often make extremely effective listeners.

4. This is a skill few, if any, people can do effectively.

5. Unfortunately, most of us need to work on improving our listening skills.

6. As human beings, we have a natural tendency to filter information we hear. All too often, what we hear is not what was said.

7. Listening is an active process. It requires our participation and involvement.

8. Our personality plays an important role in how well we listen.

9. Effective listening is done with the whole body. Proper eye contact and body posture can facilitate effective listening.

10. Feelings are often more important than the words themselves. We must look for the underlying feelings in messages. They are often the real message.

IDENTIFY CUSTOMER NEEDS
Obtain Feedback

Do you know

➤ What your customers want?

➤ What they need?

➤ What they think?

➤ How they feel?

➤ What suggestions they have?

➤ Whether they are satisfied?

A family-fun restaurant has initiated an aggressive program to solicit customer feedback. A dining room employee is assigned the task of personally asking guests at each table to fill out a feedback card. If the guests agree, the card is left at the table with a pencil. The guests deposit the card in a box at the front of the restaurant upon leaving. According to the restaurant's manager, several important improvements have been made in the operation as a result of customer suggestions. "This program has been invaluable," she states.

Question: What do a local hospital and an auto service department have in common?

Answer: They both use phone surveys to find out how satisfied their customers/patients are with the service they received.

FEEDBACK EXERCISE

Every guest service operation should have ways to obtain feedback from customers. Several methods of finding out what your customers think and feel about the services you provide are listed below. Place a check (✔)by those feedback methods that are appropriate in your situation, and discuss any questions or ideas you have with your trainer/supervisor.

Feedback methods you could use:

- ❏ Listening carefully to what customers/guests or clients have to say.

- ❏ Checking back regularly to see how things are going.

- ❏ Making feedback cards available for customers to comment on service.

- ❏ Providing a special phone number for guests, customers, and/or clients to call for questions, problems, or suggestions.

- ❏ Using a website or email address to obtain customer feedback.

- ❏ Asking other employees to solicit regular feedback when appropriate.

- ❏ Insuring the manager has regular customer contact.

- ❏ Providing a method that invites customer criticism, and then responding constructively to any complaints.

- ❏ Acknowledging all positive comments and reactions as well as any negative ones.

Other: _____

_____

My ideas for improved feedback: _____

_____

IDENTIFY CUSTOMER NEEDS
Summary and Follow-Up

Summary

The best way to identify the needs of your customers is to try and put yourself in their position, see things from their perspective, put yourself in their shoes. This section of the book has outlined a number of suggestions to help you do this.

You can identify the needs of your customers by:

➤ Knowing your customers

➤ Understanding their human needs

➤ Knowing their timing requirements

➤ Anticipating their needs in advance

➤ Being able to "read" your customers

➤ Understanding basic customer needs

➤ Practicing skillful listening

➤ Obtaining feedback

Follow-Up

If at all possible, make a visit to your operation, or one just like it at another location, as a customer. Do everything a customer would do. Make a mental note of what happens at the time and afterwards respond to the following questions.

THINGS TO DISCUSS:

1. What perspective did you develop seeing your job from the other side of the fence? _____

_____

2. How were you treated? _____

_____

3. What went well? _____

_____

4. What could have gone better? _____

_____

5. What insights did you develop that will have a positive impact on how you perform your job?_____

_____

STEP 3 PROVIDE FOR THE NEEDS OF YOUR CUSTOMERS

The most important factor in providing quality customer service is to recognize and understand all the services that your organization has available to provide.

As an assistant manager in a large retail store, Joe was frustrated with the time and inconvenience of processing customers through the check-out counters. When he finally became manager of his own store, Joe received permission from his district manager to experiment with a new check-out system. The system was so successful that it was adopted throughout the entire chain and Joe received a well-deserved promotion.

WHAT SERVICES DO YOU PROVIDE?

After each general service category, write in what you will do to provide service in that particular area. Then, add any other services you provide that have not already been listed. If you feel your response is incomplete, ask your trainer or supervisor for assistance.

1. Receiving information for customers: _____

_____

_____

2. Providing information to customers: _____

_____

_____

3. Soliciting feedback from customers: _____

_____

_____

4. Following through on customers' requests: _____

_____

_____

5. Identifying and solving problems: _____

_____

_____

6. Providing a service for customers: _____

_____

_____

7. Watching or observing: _____

_____

_____

8. Organizing: _____

_____

_____

9. Other: _____

_____

What Are the Characteristics of the Services You Provide?

Understanding your service characteristics will allow you to appreciate how the services you provide are seen by your customers.

Consider these 10 service characteristics:

1. **People/Things Orientation**

   Is the service you provide more people oriented or is it more oriented toward things (i.e., machines, equipment, and technology)?

2. **High Tech/Low Tech**

   If technology is involved in the delivery of the service provided, is it state-of-the-art, or are more traditional tools and/or systems used?

3. **Personal Interaction**

   This characteristic can be divided into three parts:

   Physical: Do the parties involved in the service have to see each other? How close are they to each other? What type of hand-off is involved?

   Mental: To what extent does the interaction demand the people involved to think, to analyze, to comprehend?

   Emotional: To what extent does the interaction rely on emotional-based-reactions and/or situations?

4. **Time Involvement**

   How long does the service take? How frequently does it occur?

5. **Location**

   Does the service take place at the customer's site, your locale, or somewhere else?

6. **Complexity**

   Actual: How complex is the service provided? How complicated are delivery systems?

   Visual: How much complexity does the customer see? Do service delivery systems appear to be simple when they are really not?

7. Accommodation

How flexible and adaptable are the service systems? To what extent can they be adjusted to meet unique or different customer needs or requests?

8. Numbers Served Per Transaction

How many customers are provided service during a single service transaction? One or two? A small group? Hundreds? Thousands?

9. Training

How much training, education, and/or expertise is needed to deliver service?

10. Supervision

How much supervision does the service system require?

DEVELOP A SERVICE PROFILE

Check (✔) the response that most closely matches the nature of the service your service team provides.

1.	People/Things Ratio	❑ More Things	❑ More People
2.	Level of Technology	❑ High Tech	❑ Low Tech
3.	Personal Interaction:		
	Physical	❑ High	❑ Low
	Mental	❑ High	❑ Low
	Emotional	❑ High	❑ Low
4.	Time Involvement:		
	Duration	❑ Long	❑ Short
	Frequency	❑ High	❑ Low
5.	Location	❑ Their Place	❑ Our Place
6.	Complexity:		
	Perception	❑ High	❑ Low
	Actual	❑ High	❑ Low
7.	Accommodation Ability	❑ High	❑ Low
8.	Numbers Served Per Transaction	❑ One	❑ Many
9.	Training required	❑ Much	❑ Little
10.	Supervision needed	❑ Much	❑ Little

How does this service profile affect the type and level of service you can provide?

_____

_____

PROVIDE FOR THE NEEDS OF YOUR CUSTOMERS
Meet Basic Needs

Four Basic Needs

The four basic needs of customers are:

1. The Need to Be Understood

2. The Need to Feel Welcome

3. The Need to Feel Important

4. The Need for Comfort

Your success on the job will depend on how well you and your organization provide for these four basic needs.

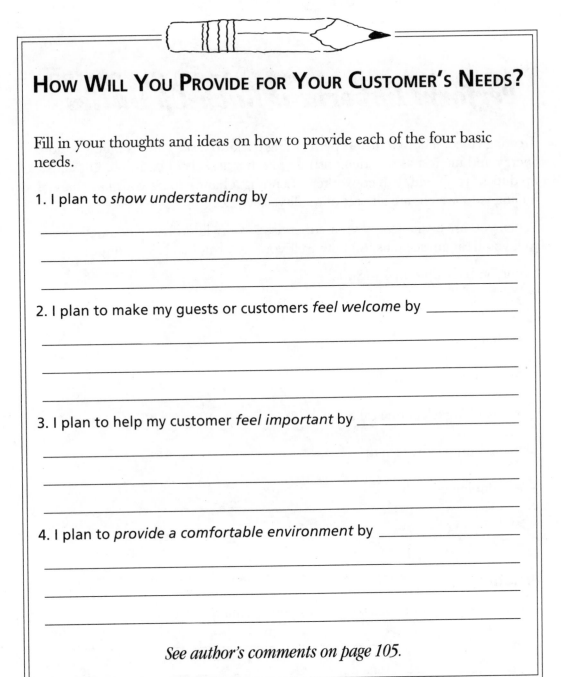

HOW WILL YOU PROVIDE FOR YOUR CUSTOMER'S NEEDS?

Fill in your thoughts and ideas on how to provide each of the four basic needs.

1. I plan to *show understanding* by _____

_____

_____

_____

2. I plan to make my guests or customers *feel welcome* by _____

_____

_____

_____

3. I plan to help my customer *feel important* by _____

_____

_____

_____

4. I plan to *provide a comfortable environment* by _____

_____

_____

_____

See author's comments on page 105.

PROVIDE FOR THE NEEDS OF YOUR CUSTOMERS
Perform Important Back-Up Duties

Treating customers well means performing back-up tasks with as much positive energy and interest as you demonstrate in other aspects of your job. Often, back-up duties are shared with co-workers. Lending a hand, doing your fair share, and pulling your weight are all part of quality service.

When you are evaluated by your supervisor, you will probably be rated on how well you treat guests, plus, on how well you perform the back-up duties.

Common back-up duties include:

➤ stocking

➤ filing

➤ recording information

➤ handling telephone calls

➤ assisting with clean-up

➤ running errands

➤ handling money

Practice

What are some of the back-up tasks you normally perform?

_____

_____

_____

_____

Check this list with your supervisor to see if you have forgotten anything critical to your job success.

PROVIDE FOR THE NEEDS OF YOUR CUSTOMERS
Send Clear Messages

Ralph runs a neighborhood bike shop. When hiring new employees for the busy fall season, he tries to tell them as much as he can about bicycles in one day. He does not spend time on training and always promises to write crucial information down, but never seems to find the time. Ralph can't understand why new employees take so long to learn the bicycle business. He laments, "I guess good help is hard to find these days."

" *Keep your message short, sweet and to the point. Be specific. Choose the small word over a big one. Work on how to express, not how to impress."*

—A Communications Expert

Do You Know How to Effectively Send a Message?

The way in which you communicate can make or break your success on the job! See if you can identify the true statements below. Check (✔) the box if the answer is true.

❏ 1. You should try to impress all customers about how knowledgeable you are.

❏ 2. You should always strive to assure the self-esteem of your guest.

❏ 3. Repeating the message back to the customer can help eliminate misunderstandings.

❏ 4. Good eye contact with a guest is rarely important.

❏ 5. When sending a message, it is important to use words that are easily understood.

❏ 6. Silence on the part of a client or guest usually indicates understanding and acceptance of your message.

❏ 7. The more you talk, the better you are at communicating.

❏ 8. Effective communication skills are inborn.

❏ 9. Following up a verbal message with a written message can often facilitate effective communication.

❏ 10. When coaching or helping a customer or fellow employee, you should focus on behavior, not on personality.

❏ 11. Your tone of voice communicates as much, or more, of the message as the words themselves.

❏ 12. Your body language sends direct messages to others regardless of what you are saying.

❏ 13. Misunderstanding a customer request is really not a serious problem.

❏ 14. Effective communication with guests or clients is more important than effective communication among fellow employees.

❏ 15. Good employees keep their supervisors well-informed at all times.

Answers: True statements are 2, 3, 5, 9, 10, 11, 12, and 15.

PROVIDE FOR THE NEEDS OF YOUR CUSTOMERS
Say the Right Thing

A 275-pound man had just finished his dinner at a local steak house when the waiter walked up and said, "Boy you made that steak disappear fast!" Later, the waiter couldn't understand why the customer complained to the manager.

Saying the Right Thing

In Step 1 of Quality Customer Service, you used your physical appearance, body language, and tone of voice to send a positive attitude.

Now, we must consider the actual words to use in order to treat customers as guests. Even though you have already communicated a great deal by your appearance and body language, it is important to complete your most effective communication skills by selecting the right words to say, and saying them in the right tone of voice.

In the space below write a script typical of your interactions with customers. Include a greeting, the words you would say to handle your transaction, and the way you would conclude the session.

Practice

My greeting would be: _____

_____

I would handle the transaction by saying: _____

_____

_____

_____

_____

_____

_____

_____

Once the business had been taken care of, I would say: _____

_____

_____

Review your choice of words with your supervisor or trainer.

PROVIDE FOR THE NEEDS OF YOUR CUSTOMERS
Sell Your Organization's Uniqueness

Beth employs three agents at her travel agency. One agent, Mary Jeanne, books more flights, cruises, and tours than all the others combined. When asked the secret to her success, Mary Jeanne commented, "All I do is make my clients aware of the alternatives available to them. I try to be enthusiastic about each option, explaining what I think is important to that client. I also look for the deals. I want clients to feel they are getting exactly what they want for the lowest price possible. I always try to make them feel good about the plan they choose. They've got to like what they buy or they simply won't come back."

Selling your customer and/or guests on the unique products and services you provide is an integral part of your job!

You sell your services by:

➤ Expanding awareness of your available services

➤ Explaining the features of these services

➤ Describing the benefits of these services

72

How Well Do You Sell Your Service?

Please list in the left-hand column below the major services you and your supervisor/trainer listed on page 60.

For each service you list in column (1), write a feature or characteristic of that service in column (2), and how that service benefits your customer and/or guests in column (3).

(1) Services available	(2) Features of service	(3) Benefits of service

The next time you mention these services remember to explain the features and benefits. Your supervisor will be favorably impressed.

PROVIDE FOR THE NEEDS OF YOUR CUSTOMERS
Meet the Computer Challenge

Most customer service positions require you to meet the needs of your customers through the use of a computer. The computer requires your attention and skill, but not at the expense of guests and/or customers. Remember, the computer is merely an object—a tool—to help you better serve your customers—human beings—with needs and wants.

COMPUTER/CUSTOMER RELATIONS EXERCISE

Five statements about computers and customer/client relations are presented below. Read each and indicate your "agreement" or "disagreement." Then, briefly explain the reasoning for your response.

Statement

1. Operating a terminal may be so difficult at first that your ability to provide quality service is adversely affected.
   ❏ **Agree**   ❏ **Disagree**   Because: _____
   _____
   _____

2. Operating the computer properly is often more important than treating a customer as a guest.
   ❏ **Agree**   ❏ **Disagree**   Because: _____
   _____
   _____

3. When you have problems with the computer, the best thing to do is to devote absolute concentration in order to work out the problem.
   ❏ **Agree**   ❏ **Disagree**   Because: _____
   _____
   _____

4. Operating a computer terminal requires you to split concentration between it and a customer/guest.
   ❏ **Agree**   ❏ **Disagree**   Because: _____
   _____
   _____

5. If your transaction is long and involved, you should always let your customer know, and then compensate by being empathetic and friendly.
   ❏ **Agree**   ❏ **Disagree**   Because: _____
   _____
   _____

Compare your comments with those of the author on page 105.

PROVIDE FOR THE NEEDS OF YOUR CUSTOMERS
Prepare for the Unexpected

Things don't always go as planned—a shipment is delayed, a key employee is ill, a newspaper ad carries an incorrect price. When the unexpected happens (and it will), the organization that is most concerned with customer service will usually come out ahead. The best approach is to think ahead to what might go wrong—and consider some back-up scenarios.

Providing quality customer service may be especially challenging when the unexpected happens. Unexpected occurrences often place extra burdens on your ability to deliver quality customer service. They may present a formidable challenge.

While all possible occurrences may not be foreseen, common, or expected, situations can be anticipated. In these cases, contingency plans can be developed to help you do your job under abnormal circumstances.

How Prepared Are You?

A number of potentially disruptive occurrences are listed below. Circle the ones that could possibly apply in your situation and then indicate any contingency action plans that could be followed to help maintain quality customer service. Discuss your ideas with your supervisor.

The Unexpected   **Your Contingency Plan**

1. Foul weather

2. Loss of power

3. Equipment failure

4. Computer breakdown

5. Overcrowded conditions

6. Understaffed

7. Fire/health emergency

8. Climate control malfunction

9. Phones out

10. Needed supplies exhausted

11. Breakdown in the delivery system

12. Other

PROVIDE FOR THE NEEDS OF YOUR CUSTOMERS
Summary

Summary

You can provide for the needs of your customers, guests, or clients by:

➤ Performing all the tasks and duties required of your job

➤ Performing important back-up duties

➤ Communicating by sending clear messages to customers, supervisors, and fellow employees

➤ Making only appropriate comments to customers

➤ Satisfying the four basic needs of your customers

➤ Practicing effective selling skills

➤ Meeting the computer challenge

➤ Continuing to deliver quality customer service when the unexpected occurs

STEP 4 MAKE SURE YOUR CUSTOMERS RETURN

Whether a customer purchases a complete wardrobe or a necktie, one medium-size department store makes it a policy to follow up each sale with a brief *thank you note*. The president of the company says, "Such a policy encourages customers to return, and that's what makes our business thrive."

Some interesting statistics* tell why companies lose customers:

➤ 1% of lost customers die

➤ 3% move away

➤ 4% just naturally float

➤ 5% change on friend's recommendations

➤ 9% can buy it cheaper somewhere else

➤ 10% are chronic complainers

➤ 68% go elsewhere because the people they deal with are indifferent to their needs

Customers are not the frosting on the cake—they *are* the cake. The frosting is an improved reputation and higher profits that are the result of quality work.

---

*Reprinted from Quality at Work.

HOW CAN YOU MAKE SURE CUSTOMERS RETURN?

Rank those items that apply to your job and then ask your supervisor
to do the same. Compare the responses and discuss any differences.

5 = Very Important   3 = Somewhat Important   1= Not Important

**Your
Ranking**   **Supervisor's
Ranking**

_____   _____   1. Always be pleasant to customers even if they are
not pleasant to you.

_____   _____   2. Welcome customer/guest suggestions about how
you could improve in your job.

_____   _____   3. Graciously receive and handle any complaints or
problems.

_____   _____   4. Go "above and beyond" to care for a customer.

_____   _____   5. Smile even during those times when you don't
feel like it.

_____   _____   6. Roll with the punches, accepting bad news and
harried schedules calmly.

_____   _____   7. Provide service that is beyond what customers
expect from you.

_____   _____   8. Provide helpful suggestions and/or guidance
when you feel customers need it.

_____   _____   9. Thoroughly explain the features and benefits for
all of the services you provide.

_____   _____   10. Follow through to ensure your customer
commitments are honored.

MAKE SURE YOUR CUSTOMERS RETURN
Handle Complaints Effectively

Statistics say it costs six times more to attract a new customer than keep a current one. Therefore, it is in your best interest and that of the organization to handle complaints to the full satisfaction of the customer.

Steps You Should Take:

1. Listen carefully to the complaint

2. Repeat the complaint back and get acknowledgment that you heard it correctly

3. Apologize

4. Acknowledge the customer's or guest's feelings (anger, frustration, disappointment, etc.)

5. Explain what action you will take to correct the problem

6. Thank the customer for bringing the problem to your attention

CASE STUDY: FRONT DESK

A guest approaches the front desk of your hotel and is visibly upset. He informs you that the room you just assigned him, is "uninhabitable" because it smells strongly of cigarette smoke. Neither he nor his wife smoke and the odor is making them nauseated. He informs you that he feels a hotel of this caliber and price should have non-smoking rooms. He demands immediate action.

CASE STUDY QUESTIONS

What would you say to this guest? _____

_____

Record your action plan below: _____

_____

Repeat the complaint: _____

_____

Apologize: _____

_____

Acknowledge the feelings: _____

_____

Explain what you will do: _____

_____

Thank the guest: _____

_____

See author comments on page 106.

COMMON COMPLAINTS

Most customer service operations find that customers tend to complain about some things more than others. Do you know what these most common complaints are? Do you know what to do and what to say when you are faced with one? Talk with your supervisor before you fill this out.

Use the left-hand column below to list the most common customer complaints you can anticipate facing on your job. For each complaint you list on the left, indicate, on the right, how you should handle the complaint. This includes what you would do and what you would say.

Common Complaints	**Recommended Action**
_____	_____
_____	_____
_____	_____
_____	_____
_____	_____
_____	_____

Dealing with Difficult People

Most difficult people are operating from a base of insecurity. Like all of us, they too, have a need to be understood, feel welcome, comfortable, and important. Difficult people are often merely expressing a need, although they are choosing an inappropriate and impolite way to communicate this need. They are being difficult for their own reasons—not because of you.

Types of difficult customers you may have to deal with:

➤ The angry customer

➤ The nasty or obnoxious person

➤ The seething, but silent individual

➤ The constant critic

➤ The nonstop talker

➤ The oddball

➤ The indecisive person

➤ The intoxicated guest

➤ The argumentative patient

Practice

What type of difficult customer do you deal with in your job?

_____

_____

Why are these people difficult? _____

_____

_____

How Well Do You Know Your Customers?

Here are some common reasons why customers may be difficult. Check (✔) the ones that may apply to you and your situation.

❑ They are tired or frustrated.

❑ They are confused or overwhelmed.

❑ They are defending their ego or self-esteem.

❑ They have never been in a similar situation before.

❑ They feel ignored. Nobody has listened to them.

❑ They may be under the influence of alcohol or drugs.

❑ They don't speak or understand the language very well.

❑ They have been treated poorly in similar circumstances in the past.

❑ They are in a bad mood and take it out on you.

❑ They are in a hurry or have waited an extended period of time for service.

❑ Other (you specify) _____

_____

MAKE SURE YOUR CUSTOMERS RETURN
Get Difficult Customers on Your Side

1. Don't take it personally.

This is one of the hardest customer service skills to learn. Remember, difficult customers are not attacking you personally (even though it may seem that they are).

2. Remain calm. Listen carefully.

This is easy to say here, but difficult to do. Take a deep breath and plan your words carefully. Paraphrase what customers have said to make sure you have heard them correctly.

3. Focus on the problem, not the person.

Go to a quiet area. Sit down. Be a problem-solver. Try to figure out what this person needs and satisfy this need in some way, if you can. Let the customer know what you can do.

4. Reward yourself for turning a difficult customer into a happy one.

Smile. Pat yourself on the back. Know that you have accomplished an amazing feat. You are a customer service hero.

5. When all else fails, ask for help.

When you find yourself confronted with a difficult situation you don't know how to handle, involve your supervisor. Certain problems may require your supervisor to handle them. If so, find out what these problem areas are, and observe how they are handled.

CASE STUDY: AIRLINE TICKET COUNTER

A woman approaches the ticket counter of an airline at a large airport and demands to see the manager. You ask if you can be of any assistance since the manager is not available. She immediately challenges the airline's no pet policy as unfair and discriminatory. She explains that she has to travel 1000 miles to attend a sick sister. Her toy poodle, with whom she has never been separated, is completely house broken and "never barks or bites." She can't stand the thought of her "little baby" all alone in the dangerous, cold and dark baggage compartment. After all, "dogs can freeze in there and there may not be enough air to breathe." She is holding the dog tightly in her arms. The pooch is clothed in a designer jacket made for small dogs and has her nails polished bright red. The lady loudly demands she be allowed to bring her pet onboard with her.

CONTINUED

CONTINUED **CASE STUDY QUESTIONS**

What should you do? Place a check (✔) in the box of the actions below that are the most appropriate response to this difficult situation:

❏ 1. Show slight disgust on your face so she will know you consider her to be the problem.

❏ 2. Laugh and make light of the situation.

❏ 3. Remain calm, cool, and patient.

❏ 4. Sympathize with her feelings of fear and frustration. Tell her that you don't like to leave your pets alone either.

❏ 5. Walk away to find the manager.

❏ 6. Become distant and less cooperative.

❏ 7. Disarm her by asking, "Are you serious?"

❏ 8. Explain carefully about the gentle treatment pets receive in the pet compartment and how many pets fly your airline each day.

❏ 9. Ask her to understand the airline's need to consider all the passengers.

❏ 10. Thank her for understanding and cooperating.

See comments of author on page 106.

MAKE SURE YOUR CUSTOMERS RETURN
Take That One Extra Service Step

Patty, a part-time employee in a neighborhood gift shop, was helping a young woman in a hurry. While the woman was looking for the right gift card, Patty was wrapping the gift to which the card would be attached. Suddenly Patty realized that the customer was taking the gift directly from the store to the recipient and said, "I'll bet you will need a pen to sign the card. Here, take this one with you." The customer said in surprise, "Yes. How did you know? Thank you very much."

Surprise Your Customers!

You will find your level of quality customer service growing if you learn how to treat all of your customers as guests. Learn to go the extra mile. Go beyond what they expect!

Examples:

Ticket Agent: *"Would you like me to select a seat for your return flight at this time?"*

Salesperson: *"I'll deliver it personally this afternoon."*

Night nurse: *"Since you are awake, would you like something to drink?"*

Loan officer: *"I don't know the answer now, but I'll call you back before 11:00 A.M. with the answer."*

Food Server: *"May I bring an extra plate so you two can share this special dessert?"*

Hotel desk clerk: *"May I call a cab for you?"*

Auto mechanic: *"Since your repairs will take longer than planned, may I give you a lift home?"*

Receptionist in a state agency: *"To avoid getting lost on the third floor, let me draw a map for you."*

Grocery clerk: *"Let me get you some help carrying out your groceries."*

Bank clerk: *"Would you like a new checkbook cover, free of charge?"*

Practice

How can you take that extra step of service?

_____

_____

_____

HOW CAN YOU GO THE EXTRA STEP?

List ways you feel would be appropriate for you to go the extra mile in your job. Then, share the list with your supervisor.

1. _____

_____

2. _____

_____

3. _____

_____

4. _____

_____

5. _____

_____

6. _____

_____

7. _____

_____

8. _____

_____

9. _____

_____

10. _____

_____

MAKE SURE YOUR CUSTOMERS RETURN
Summary

Summary

Make sure your customers, clients, or guests return by:

➤ Working to satisfy customer complaints

➤ Being prepared to properly handle the most common complaints

➤ Learning to get difficult customers on your side

➤ Understanding why some customers are more difficult than others

➤ Taking that one extra step to provide quality customer service

➤ Consistently practicing all the principles of quality customer service that you have learned about in this book

P A R T 3

Notes and
Comments

CHECK YOUR CUSTOMER SERVICE KNOWLEDGE

True or False?

❏ T ❏ F 1. People who are successful at customer relations constantly need to be the center of attention.

❏ T ❏ F 2. Treating customers as guests means viewing your job primarily as a human relations representative.

❏ T ❏ F 3. Customer service employees are at the mercy of their customers, and thus, have little control over their success on the job.

❏ T ❏ F 4. Treating customers as guests often means apologizing for mistakes you did not make.

❏ T ❏ F 5. It really isn't important to remember the names and faces of your customers.

❏ T ❏ F 6. If you have limited desire to please others, you probably shouldn't be in a service related job.

❏ T ❏ F 7. How you handle the procedural (or technical) side of your job can directly affect how you handle the personal side.

❏ T ❏ F 8. Knowing the time requirements for providing quality service will help you do a better job.

❏ T ❏ F 9. Anticipating needs means providing items and services for customers without requiring them to ask.

❏ T ❏ F 10. When communicating with another person, it is important to always consider and protect his or her self-esteem.

❏ T ❏ F 11. Eye contact has little impact on good communication.

❏ T ❏ F 12. Feedback rarely provides the information necessary to do a better job.

CONTINUED

CONTINUED

❏ T ❏ F 13. If you are not careful, working on a computer can adversely affect your attentiveness toward customers/guests.

❏ T ❏ F 14. Generally, the attitude you receive from others is the same attitude you transmit.

❏ T ❏ F 15. Reading the customer correctly can pay great dividends for you and your organization.

❏ T ❏ F 16. Most people simply want fast service and have little need to feel important or be recognized.

❏ T ❏ F 17. Body language often communicates more than the actual words you use.

❏ T ❏ F 18. When a guest is rude, obnoxious, and impolite, it is justifiable for you to return the same behavior.

❏ T ❏ F 19. It is really impractical to think that you should try to go one step beyond the expectations of those you serve.

❏ T ❏ F 20. Customer complaints should be encouraged.

Answers on page 106.

Assess Your Customer Service Skills

How close are you to being a customer service winner?

The *Service Provider Self-Assessment Scale* (SP SAS) provides an opportunity for you to assess your customer service skills. It is a useful tool to evaluate the progress you are making toward providing a quality level of service to your customers.

Using the five-point scale for each question, you can judge how frequently you exhibit 15 specific quality service behaviors. This allows you to identify your service strengths as well as your weaknesses.

Scores less than 100% for a given category represent opportunities for improving your customer service effectiveness and joining the ranks of the thousands of fellow service providers who have mastered these winning customer service techniques.

SERVICE PROVIDER
SELF-ASSESSMENT SCALE (SP SAS)

Answer each question according to how often you actually exhibit the described behavior.

4 = Always   3 = Mostly   2 = Sometimes   1 = Rarely   0 = Never

DO YOU...

_____ 1. Consistently provide service in a timely manner compatible with customer needs?

_____ 2. Provide guests, who are waiting for service, something to occupy their time while waiting?

_____ 3. Keep the sequence of service steps flowing smoothly and incrementally?

_____ 4. Know and deal with customer service needs in order of priority?

_____ 5. Keep one step ahead of customer needs?

_____ 6. Provide needed service to customers before they have to ask for it?

_____ 7. Orally repeat customer orders or requests back to them?

_____ 8. Communicate with fellow service team members in a timely, accurate, and thorough manner?

_____ 9. Ask specific questions when seeking feedback from customers?

_____ 10. Provide a mechanism for customer feedback other than an oral response?

_____ 11. Say "yes" to unusual or special customer requests?

_____ 12. Offer a convenience to customers that may be an inconvenience to you?

_____ 13. Work well under little or no supervision?

_____ 14. Work in an organized and efficient manner?

_____ 15. Display nothing but positive attitudes on the job?

_____ 16. Provide service with a smile?

_____ 17. Reflect a customer-friendly tone of voice?

_____ 18. Display enthusiasm toward the job?

_____ 19. Use polite and tactful words when speaking to customers?

_____ 20. Avoid using slang or jargon when speaking to customers?

_____ 21. Follow a system that facilitates the use of customer names?

_____ 22. Refer to customers by name when providing or concluding service?

_____ 23. Provide that "extra touch" when assisting customers?

_____ 24. Individualize service to customers when necessary?

_____ 25. Answer all customer questions about products and/or services?

_____ 26. Provide helpful suggestions to customers?

_____ 27. Use effective selling skills?

_____ 28. Mention product and/or service upgrades?

_____ 29. Remain pleasant and calm when customers are upset, angry, or hostile?

_____ 30. Graciously handle complaints to the customer's satisfaction?

SCORING THE SP SAS

In each category, record the number you wrote for each of the corresponding questions. The resulting percentages will show you your strengths and opportunities for improvement. If you have a lower percentage on a certain skill, that is a good indication that you could benefit from improvement in that area.

EXAMPLE

Timeliness: 1 _4_ 2 _4_

Total _8_ /8 = _100_ %

Timeliness: 1 _____ 2_____

Total _____/8 = _____%

Incremental Flow: 3 _____ 4_____

Total _____/8 = _____%

Anticipation: 5 _____ 6 _____

Total _____/8 = _____%

Communication: 7 _____ 8 _____

Total _____/8 = _____%

Customer Feedback: 9 _____ 10_____

Total _____/8 = _____%

Accommodation: 11_____ 12_____

Total _____/8 = _____%

Organization/Supervision: 13_____   14_____

                                 Total _____/8 = _____%

Attitude/Body Language: 15_____   16_____

                                 Total _____/8 = _____%

Attitude/Tone of Voice: 17_____   18_____

                                 Total _____/8 = _____%

Tact: 19_____   20_____

                                 Total _____/8 = _____%

Naming Names: 21_____   22_____

                                 Total _____/8 = _____%

Attentiveness: 23_____   24_____

                                 Total _____/8 = _____%

Guidance: 25_____   26_____

                                 Total _____/8 = _____%

Selling Skills: 27_____   28_____

                                 Total _____/8 = _____%

Gracious Problem Solving: 29_____   30_____

                                 Total _____/8 = _____%

Conclusion

You have now completed this program. This is an excellent time to sit down with your manager and/or trainer and talk about what you have learned. This is also a good time to clarify any questions you may have about the job.

Tell your manager you have completed the program and arrange a meeting. Use the space below to make notes about what you want to talk about or questions you still have.

THINGS TO DISCUSS: ————————————————————————

1. _____

2. _____

3. _____

4. _____

5. _____

6. _____

Author's Notes and Comments

Body Language Exercise (p.28)

Positive Messages:

Face is relaxed and under control.
This communicates you are prepared, know what you are doing, and/or are comfortable with your role.

Smile is natural and comfortable.
This communicates you are sure of yourself, like what you are doing, and enjoy your guests.

Eye contact is maintained when talking and listening with guests.
This communicates guests are important, you are interested in them and, are self-confident.

Body movement is deliberate and controlled.
This communicates you are in control, you are glad to be where you are, and that although busy that's just part of the job.

Negative Messages:

Face is anxious and uptight.
This communicates you are ill prepared, inexperienced, and/or uncomfortable with your role.

Smile is forced or phony.
This communicates you are unsure of yourself, don't like what you are doing, and/or really don't enjoy your guests.

Eye contact is avoided when talking and listening to customers.
This communicates a lack of interest in guest, and/or you lack the self-confidence to do the job.

Body movement is harried and rushed.
This communicates you are not in control of the situation, and would really like the guests to leave.

How Well Do You Use Your Voice? (p.30)

The tone of voice that is conducive to your success in customer relations can be described by any of these four characteristics:

1. It is upbeat.
2. It is warm, comfortable, and understanding.
3. It is under control.
4. It is clear, direct, and natural.

Case Study: Thelma's Performance Appraisal (p.36)

1. Is Thelma a good employee? *Answer*: Both "yes and "no." She certainly does half of her job well–the non-people side. When it comes to interacting with customers, a very important part of the job, Thelma is not a good employee.

2. Is the manager justified in his recommendations? *Answer*: I think so. He cannot afford someone like Thelma turning off customers. His business relies on warm, friendly customer relations.

3. What suggestions would you make to Thelma? *Answer*: Learn and practice the principles of quality customer service as soon as possible or seek a position in the restaurant or elsewhere that won't require customer interaction.

How Timely Should You Be? (p.46)

The value of this exercise is to establish clear timeliness expectations between you and your supervisor or trainer and your customers. You may have your own ideas of what is timely, but it is more important to find out what your *supervisor and customers* consider to be timely. In fact, your job may depend upon it.

How Well Do You Anticipate Customer Needs? (p.48)

Situation:	Anticipated Need:
1. A customer has waited longer than normal for service.	An extra warm smile. A verbal recognition of the extended wait. A comment of appreciation for waiting. Speedy service.
2. A client keeps glancing at his watch.	This person may have a plane to catch or another appointment. Recognize this need and provide timely service.
3. A women guest with three small children approaches your service area.	Provide some items to occupy the children while they wait.
4. Lines for service form early in the day.	Have appropriate supplies and equipment on hand. Have enough staff to meet the demand.
5. You have well-defined busy periods in your workday.	Prepare yourself mentally and physically. Don't be caught off guard.

How Well Do You Read Your Customers? (p.50)

Signal:		Possible Customer Need:
Age of customer:	*Young:*	Some young customers may be inexperienced or unsure of themselves. Explain things clearly. Be patient and set them at ease.
	Elderly:	Seniors appreciate a friendly comment or two. Make casual conversation. Show some interest and attention.
Type of clothing:	*High fashion:*	Show well-dressed people the respect and deference they expect.
	Out of fashion:	Help these people feel welcome and comfortable.
	Worn Out:	These people may be careful with their money. Respect that and make them feel welcome.
Verbal ability:	*Extremely fluent:*	Listen carefully. Paraphrase back what you hear.
	Barely fluent:	Be patient and match your speaking pace with the customer's.
Attitude:	*Positive:*	Recognize and encourage it.
	Negative:	Be positive and understanding. Show empathy.
Impatient:		Be as timely as you can be. Explain what's happening. Explain how long the process will take. Be polite.
Demanding or angry:		Be polite and patient. Listen carefully. Stay calm. Show understanding.

How Do Your Customers Signal These Needs to You? (p.51)

Customers express these four needs in a variety of way. Here are just a few of them.

The Need to be Understood. This need is signaled by customers repeating themselves, speaking slowly, speaking loudly, getting angry when they are not being understood, or bringing a friend or relative to help explain.

The Need to Feel Welcome. This need is signaled by "looking around" before coming in and/or coming in with friends or relatives. It is also demonstrated by wearing the "right" clothes for the situation.

The Need to Feel Important. This need is often signaled by someone "showing off" or bragging about who they know. This need is also demonstrated by flashing money, a display of jewelry, and/or extreme clothing.

The Need for Comfort. This need is expressed by customers being ill at ease, nervous, or unsure of themselves when feeling uncomfortable. This need is also expressed when help, assistance, or directions are requested.

How Will You Provide for Your Customer's Needs? (p.65)

1. Need to be Understood. Paraphrase back what is being said. Listen for feelings communicated as well as the content of the message. Empathize with problems or predicaments.

2. Need to Feel Welcome. Provide a warm and friendly welcome. Talk in a language everyone will understand. Engage in friendly conversation.

3. Need to Feel Important. Learn to call others by name. Do something special. Tune in to individual needs.

4. Need for Comfort. Set customers at ease. Relieve anxiety. Explain the service procedures carefully and calmly.

Computer/Customer Relations Exercise (p.74)

1. *Agree.* **Because:** You may sacrifice valuable customer time getting the computer to work properly. If you can practice on the computer before hours or during slow periods, this problem should be minimized.

2. *Disagree.* **Because:** You must learn to treat customers as guests and operate the computer properly. Both are vital to your job success.

3. *Disagree.* **Because:** Never concentrate on a computer problem at the expense of a customer. Get some assistance right away.

4. *Agree.* **Because:** This is true; however, operating the computer soon becomes second nature. When this happens, you will be able to focus the majority of your attention on the customers.

5. *Agree.* **Because:** Always let your client know what is going on. Sometimes a wait or delay doesn't seem quite as long when you have received an explanation for the delay.

106

Case Study: Front Desk (p.81)

A possible dialogue might go something like this:

Clerk: "Your room smells strongly of cigarette smoke." (Repeating the complaint). "I'm very sorry, sir," (Apology). "You certainly have a right to be upset. I would be too." (Acknowledgment of feelings). "What I would like to do, if it is okay with you, is move you and your wife to another room right away. I'll have a bellman assist you." (Explaining the action that you will take). "Would that be all right?"

Guest: "Much better."

Clerk: "Thank you for bringing this my attention. I'm glad you told me about it. It should not have happened." (Thanking the guest).

Case Study: Airline Ticket Counter (p.86)

The correct responses to this situation would be to:

3. Remain calm, cool, and patient.

4. Recognize the feelings of frustration and fear she expressed by telling her that you don't like to leave your pets alone either.

8. Tell her about the gentle treatment pets receive in the pet compartment and how many pets fly your airline each day.

10. Thank her for understanding and cooperating.

Check Your Customer Service Knowledge (p.95–96)

1. **F** (Treating customers as guests means to make them the center of attention.) 2. **T** 3. **F** (You have almost complete control over your job success.) 4. **T** 5. **F** (Remembering names and faces is one of the most important things you can do.) 6. **T** 7. **T** 8. **T** 9. **T** 10. **T** 11. **F** (Eye contact has a great impact on communication.) 12. **F** (Member feedback provides invaluable information.) 13. **T** 14. **T** 15. **T** 16. **F** (Most members want to be served quickly and efficiently, and need to feel important and recognized.) 17. **T** 18. **F** (It is never justifiable to be rude or short with a guest.) 19. **F** (Going one step beyond the expectations of your guests should become a natural extension of your job.) 20. **T**.

Additional Reading

Anderson, Kristin and Ron Zemke. *Delivering Knock Your Socks Off Service.* New York: American Management Association, 1998.

Barlow, Janelle, Dianna Maul, and Michael Edwardson. *Emotional Value: Creating Strong Bonds with Your Customers.* San Francisco: Berrett-Koehler Publishers, Inc., 2000.

Bell, Chip R. *Customers as Partners: Building Relationships That Last.* San Francisco: Berrett-Koehler Publishers, 1994.

Blanchard, Ken and Sheldon Bowles. *Raving Fans: A Revolutionary Approach to Customer Service.* New York: William Morrow & Company, Inc., 1993.

Davidow, William H. and Bro Uttal. *Total Customer Satisfaction: The Ultimate Weapon.* New York: HarperCollins, 1990.

Gitomer, Jeffrey. *Customer Satisfaction Is Worthless, Customer Loyalty Is Priceless.* Austin: Bard Press, 1998.

Greiner, Donna and Theodore B. Kinn. *1,001 Ways to Keep Customers Coming Back.* Rocklin, CA.: Prima Publishing, 1999.

Griffin, Jill, *Customer Loyalty. How to Earn It, How to Keep It.* San Francisco: Jossey-Bass Publishers, 1995.

Gross, T. Scott. *Positively Outrageous Service.* New York: Warner Books, 1991.

Karr, Ron and Don Blohowiak. *The Complete Idiot's Guide to Great Customer Service.* New York: Alpha Books, 1997.

LeBoeuf, Michael. *How to Win Customers and Keep Them for Life.* New York: Berkley Books, 1989.

Leland, Karen and Keith Bailey. *Customer Service for Dummies.* Foster City, CA: IDG Books, 1995.

Martin, William B.. *Managing Quality Customer Service.* Menlo Park, CA: Crisp Publications, 1989.

Sanders, Betsy. *Fabled Service, Ordinary Acts, Extraordinary Outcomes.* San Francisco: Jossey-Bass Publishers, 1995.

Willingham, Ron. *Hey, I'm The Customer.* Paramus, NJ: Prentice Hall, 1992.

To the Supervisor and/or Trainer

Quality Customer Service has been designed to make your job as a trainer more effective, and hopefully a bit easier. This book is not intended to replace on-the-job training. Its purpose is to set the stage for more efficient hands-on training.

Flexibility

This book breaks winning with the customer into four simple steps:

Step 1: Transmit a Positive Attitude
Step 2: Identify Customer Needs
Step 3: Provide for Customer Needs
Step 4: Make Sure Customers Return

Ideally the trainee will complete each step before actual customer contact, although these learning steps can be used effectively at any time.

If you are using *Quality Customer Service* to complement other training that is taking place, each step may be assigned independently or in concert with other sessions. The program is highly adaptable and can be used with most training programs.

Feedback and Discussion

Trainees will want to discuss the exercises in this book. Questions will arise that only you can answer. The following sections in the book suggest your involvement.

1. A discussion of the case, "Thelma's Performance Appraisal," (page 36 is helpful and will serve as a general review of Step 1: Transmit a Positive Attitude.

2. The "How Timely Should You Be?" exercise on page 46 asks for your input based on the specific timing requirements of your organization.

3. The trainee may need help listing all of the services he/she will be providing as well as services provided by others on page 60. You may also want to review the trainee's script for handling a customer transaction on page 70.

4. Following pages 80 and 81 you may wish to discuss the policies and procedures you may have for handling customer complaints or difficult guests.

Upon Completion of the Program

A follow-up session between you and the trainee is suggested at the end of the program. To make the session most effective, you should arrange a meeting and discuss each section of the book. The feedback that follows should help you establish a supportive relationship with your service provider. The time you devote to these sessions will be well invested.

Note: The author of this book has written a similar work for supervisors and/or trainers titled *Managing Quality Customer Service*. It is also in the *Fifty-Minute™ Series* and filled with helpful tips, examples, and worksheets aimed at those responsible for managing a quality program. For more information on this book call Crisp Publications, Inc. at 1-800-442-7477.

NOTES

Now Available From

CRiSP Learning

Books • Videos • CD-ROMs • Computer-Based Training Products

Subject Areas Include:

Management
Human Resources
Communication Skills
Personal Development
Marketing/Sales
Organizational Development
Customer Service/Quality
Computer Skills
Small Business and Entrepreneurship
Adult Literacy and Learning
Life Planning and Retirement

⟩ WORLDWIDE DISTRIBUTION

are distributed worldwide. Major international distributors include:

ASIA/PACIFIC

Australia/New Zealand: In Learning, PO Box 1051, Springwood QLD, Brisbane, Australia 4127   Tel: 61-7-3-841-2286, Facsimile: 61-7-3-841-1580
ATTN: Messrs. Richard/Robert Gordon

Hong Kong/Mainland China: Crisp Learning Solutions, 18/F Honest Motors Building 9-11 Leighton Rd., Causeway Bay, Hong Kong   Tel: 852-2915-7119, Facsimile: 852-2865-2815 ATTN: Ms. Grace Lee

Indonesia: Pt Lutan Edukasi, Citra Graha, 7th Floor, Suite 701A, Jl. Jend. Gato Subroto Kav. 35-36, Jakarta 12950 Indonesia Tel: 62-21-527-9060/527-9061 Facsimile: 62-21-527-9062 ATTN: Mr. Suwardi Luis

Japan: Phoenix Associates, Believe Mita Bldg., 8th Floor 3-43-16 Shiba, Minato-ku, Tokyo 105-0014, Japan   Tel: 81-3-5427-6231, Facsimile: 81-3-5427-6232
ATTN: Mr. Peter Owans

Malaysia, Philippines, Singapore: Epsys Pte Ltd., 540 Sims Ave #04-01, Sims Avenue Centre, 387603, Singapore   Tel: 65-747-1964, Facsimile: 65-747-0162 ATTN: Mr. Jack Chin

CANADA

Crisp Learning Canada, 60 Briarwood Avenue, Mississauga, ON L5G 3N6 Canada Tel: 905-274-5678, Facsimile: 905-278-2801 ATTN: Mr. Steve Connolly

EUROPEAN UNION

England: Flex Learning Media, Ltd., 9-15 Hitchin Street, Baldock, Hertfordshire, SG7 6AL, England Tel: 44-1-46-289-6000, Facsimile: 44-1-46-289-2417   ATTN: Mr. David Willetts

INDIA

Multi-Media HRD, Pvt. Ltd., National House, Floor 1, 6 Tulloch Road, Appolo Bunder, Bombay, India 400-039 Tel: 91-22-204-2281, Facsimile: 91-22-283-6478 ATTN: Messrs. Ajay Aggarwal/ C.L. Aggarwal

SOUTH AMERICA

Mexico: Grupo Editorial Iberoamerica, Nebraska 199, Col. Napoles, 03810 Mexico, D.F. Tel: 525-523-0994, Facsimile: 525-543-1173   ATTN: Señor Nicholas Grepe

SOUTH AFRICA

Corporate: Learning Resources, PO Box 2806, Parklands, Johannesburg 2121, South Africa, Tel: 27-21-531-2923, Facsimile: 27-21-531-2944 ATTN: Mr. Ricky Robinson

MIDDLE EAST

Edutech Middle East, L.L.C., PO Box 52334, Dubai U.A.E. Tel: 971-4-359-1222, Facsimile: 971-4-359-6500   ATTN: Mr. A.S.F. Karim